# EUROPEAN TRAMS

## A PICTORIAL SURVEY

L. F. FOLKARD

# D. BRADFORD BARTON LTD

**Frontispiece:** A pre-war Rome bogie car on a section of private track near the Colosseum, which can be seen in the background. These well-maintained veterans comprise over half of the Rome tram fleet, and new articulated cars are on order with which it is planned to reopen a closed route in 1976.

 © copyright D. Bradford Barton 1976          ISBN 0 85153 280 2

printed in Great Britain by H. E. Warne Ltd, London and St. Austell

for the publishers

**D. BRADFORD BARTON LTD · Trethellan House · Truro · Cornwall · England**

# CONTENTS

# INTRODUCTION

Many European countries rely to a large extent on the electric tram for public transport in their towns and cities, and a good variety of different types in colourful liveries is to be found at work in all sorts of environments, ranging from huge city systems such as those at Vienna and Leningrad to isolated rural lines tucked away among the mountains of Switzerland and Italy, the lakes of Austria, the plains of the Danube, and the forests of the Ardennes.

To set the stage by giving a perforce very brief introduction to the subject, horse tramways came to Europe in the 1860s – though New York had them in 1832 – and steam traction was tried in the later years of the century. The first electric street tramway ran (in Berlin) in 1881, and cable-hauled trams found favour in a few places, usually where the hills were too steep for horses to cope with. By the early years of the present century, most European cities and towns of any importance had electric tramways.

It is not proposed to go into the reasons for the tram's fall from favour in Britain, but although so few remain, we are fortunate inasmuch as three forms of traction can still be found in public service – electric at Blackpool, cable at Llandudno and horse at Douglas. In addition, the tramway museum at Crich in Derbyshire is strongly recommended, for here one can see and ride on trams which used to operate on many British systems, Sheffield and Glasgow being particularly well represented.

Despite their share of closures, many tram systems on the Continent have been redeveloped to suit present-day traffic conditions by extensive use of reserved and private tracks, some in subway, and equipped with a new generation of fast, quiet-running trams. There may indeed still be a future for the modern tram in Britain, as the Tyne & Wear Metro, now under construction, shows every indication of being very similar to the type of system to which some of the more progressive German tramways have already evolved.

The traditional double-decker was never generally favoured on the Continent, and until the post-war years most tramways used small single-deckers towing one or two trailers. These are now themselves fast becoming a rarity, having been supplanted by high-capacity bogie or articulated cars. Continental practice has long been to provide a comparatively small number of seats but plenty of standing room, for instance many trams can now carry well over 200 passengers with a crew of just one – the driver. To achieve this end, pre-purchased tickets are often the rule, with a small army of plain-clothes inspectors to administer instant justice where necessary.

The illustrations in this book have been selected with the object of presenting typical examples of the trams to be found in Europe over the last fifteen years or so, the period which followed the closure of the major British tram systems and during which many railway and tramway enthusiasts first turned their cameras towards the good things that awaited them across the Channel.

Grateful thanks are due to those who have supplied photographs, in particular to Michael Taplin (Overseas News Editor of 'Modern Tramway') and to Peter Gray (better known for his railway photographs). Where no credit is shown, the illustration is by the Editor.

Leslie F. Folkard
Torquay

**GREAT BRITAIN** The only remaining electric street tramway system in Britain is at Blackpool, whose one route runs along the whole length of the promenade, almost entirely on paved reserved track at the side of the road. Then it runs across country to Fleetwood, where it passes through the streets in the traditional manner. The service is strengthened by short workings on the promenade section, where No.708 is seen on its way to the terminus at Starr Gate. Blackpool also operates single-deck trams and a few trailers.

A busy scene in Glasgow in 1958, with trams of three types in Argyle Street. Bogie car No.1151 is one of the 'Coronation' type, built from 1937 onwards; No.1005 is interesting in that it started life in 1947 as an experimental single-ended car, a comparative rarity in Britain, but was later rebuilt conventionally with controls at each end. No.283 which follows it is one of Glasgow's standard four-wheel cars, of which there were once a thousand. The last Glasgow route closed in 1962.

The Tramway Museum at Crich in Derbyshire houses about 40 trams, mostly in working order and restored to a high standard. On busy days, several cars operate on the museum's ¾-mile route, and in this photograph Sheffield No.510 and Glasgow No.812 are loading.

Britain's newest tramway is in Devon, and runs from Seaton to Colyford mainly on the trackbed of the closed B R branch line. It is built to 2ft.9in. gauge and most of its rolling stock previously operated on a short line at Eastbourne. The fleet consists of four open-top double deckers which are built to just over half normal size, plus No.12 which is a solitary enclosed single decker. Further cars are in the course of building or rebuilding, and all contain parts from scrapped full-size trams.

One of the famous horse trams in front of its depot at Douglas, Isle of Man. Their route runs the length of the promenade, and they are almost certainly the last horse trams operating a service along public roads anywhere in the world. The tramway celebrates its centenary in 1976.

A cable tramway runs from Llandudno up the steep hill to the Great Orme, being operated in two sections with a winding house halfway driving the two cables with two cars on each. The overhead wires and trolleys are purely for communication purposes and the cars have no lights and no glass in the saloon windows. The lower section of the line runs through the street and the cable is located under the surface, while the top section is cross-country with the cable exposed. More sophisticated cable trams ran in Edinburgh until 1924, and of course San Francisco retains two much-publicised routes.

The Manx Electric Railway runs northward from Douglas on a highly scenic route, and most of its fleet is between 70 and 80 years old. A fascinating glimpse of some of these venerable cars is seen in the depot at Douglas, not far from the horse tram terminus.

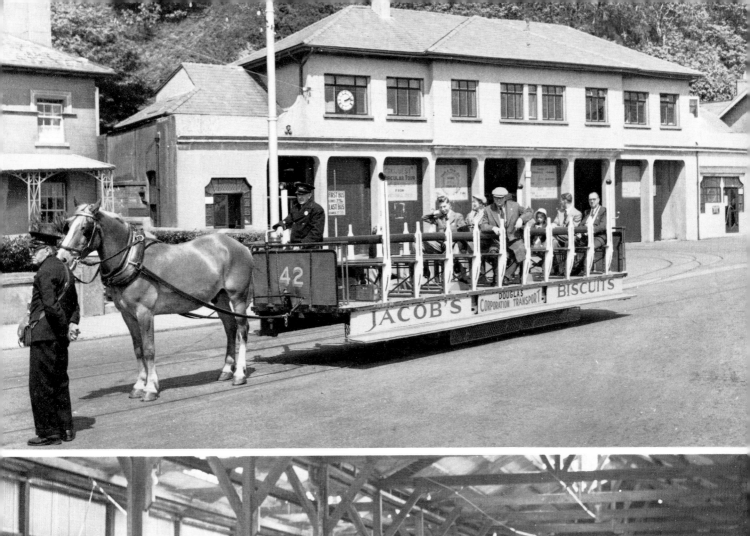

**IRELAND** The last electric tramway in Ireland was the Hill of Howth line, not far from Dublin, which closed in 1959. The photograph depicts a typical section of the route as seen from one of the open-top double-deckers.

The Valenciennes system, whose last trams ran in 1966, served an area of mining communities, and some routes went as far as the Belgian border. Car No.24 with open-platform trailers is seen at Bon Secours terminus in no-mans-land between the French and Belgian frontier posts.

**FRANCE** Only a few tramways remain in France, one of the survivors being the SNELRT, which runs from Lille to Roubaix and Tourcoing near the Belgian border. Bogie car No.525 is seen at Roubaix.

**SPAIN** Seen in front of the Puerta de Toledo, Madrid bogie car No.1015 was one of 160 built in the 1940s and 1950s by the Italian Fiat company. These modern cars were not enough to prevent the final closure of the Madrid tramways in 1972.

The 750mm-gauge Granada-Sierra Nevada tramway was probably the most spectacular in Europe. After leaving Granada along the side of a country road, it suddenly took a tortuous course up into the mountains, along narrow shelves with a sheer drop down to the river, across ravines, and through tunnels. After many years of being subsidised by the state, it was most regrettably closed early in 1974. The last surviving metre-gauge routes of the Granada tramways closed about the same time. Sierra Nevada car No.4 is depicted at El Charcón in 1966.                                                                                    [P. W. Gray]

The industrial town and port of Gijon, on Spain's northern coast, operated wooden-bodied trams over poorly-maintained track until the system closed in 1964. Some of the crews here objected to photographs being taken, perhaps out of embarrassment!

Barcelona operated a few double-deckers until 1963, and was the last undertaking in continental Europe to do so. No.205 probably never carried another passenger after this photograph was taken, though much of the Barcelona tram system remained until the late 1960s, worked by a great variety of single deckers. Final closure took place in 1971 – nowhere in Europe have recent years taken such a heavy toll of tramways as in Spain, a country which in 1960 had so much to offer the enthusiast but now has so little.

**PORTUGAL** Lisbon still has a sizeable tram system, laid to the narrow gauge of 900mm. The first generation of cars were all American-built, and No.330 of 1906, although rebuilt with air brakes in 1931/2, retained most of its original features when photographed at Santa Apolonia in 1964. Note the 'maximum traction' bogies, each having two large and two small wheels. The motors drive on to the axles with the large wheels, and the bogie pivot is over these axles. Several of Lisbon's routes negotiate extremely steep and narrow streets, necessitating the use of small four wheel cars.

Oporto No.178 dates from the 1920s, and is a locally-built product to the design of the J. G. Brill Company in U.S.A., who had previously supplied similar cars. It is of the 'semi-convertible' type, having saloon windows which retract completely up into the roof. The sloping fairing between the fender and the dash is an 'anti-climber', fitted to deter passengers from riding outside the car – although some still do!

The picturesque and hilly university town of Coimbra, 115 miles north of Lisbon, has an unusual little tram system consisting principally of one-way circular routes, operated by twenty assorted four-wheel cars several of which have bodies built locally. In the photograph, Nos.12 and 18 have just passed under an aqueduct.  [P. W. Gray]

The Gloria Elevador at Lisbon. The two cars which operate on this steep hill are counterbalanced on a cable which runs under the road, but the actual drive is through electric motors mounted on the cars themselves, which have horizontal bodies carried on inclined frames.

23

The Boa Vista depot of the Oporto tramways with Belgian-built bogie cars visible on the left and locally-built four-wheelers elsewhere. Other Oporto cars are American-built and are much sought after by museums in the U.S.A. Several have already been exported, but others have to be retained as a sizeable part of the system is still running. [P. W. Gray]

**BELGIUM** Brussels No.7091, built in 1957 on secondhand American 'PCC' type bogies, approaches the city streets from the private track near the Exhibition ground. In the background is the Atomium, built for the 1958 Exposition. Much of the tramway in central Brussels is now in subway, with a view to eventual operation as a Metro system.

The articulated car developed for use in Brussels, also on American-type 'PCC' trucks built under licence in Belgium. No.7504 has just come up from one of the subways, the approach ramp to which is visible on the right. A few very similar cars were supplied to St. Etienne in France.

Metre-gauge Belgian Vicinal 'N' class bogie cars at Wemmel tram station, on the outskirts of Brussels. Most of this type of car have either been converted to trailers or sold to Spain, but more powerful cars operate Vicinal services in the Charleroi area and on the coastal routes centred at Ostend, as well as on the two routes which still penetrate into Brussels.

A diesel tram with saloon and open trailers on the Han-sur-Lesse to Grottes de Han line in the Ardennes, which operates solely to take visitors to the celebrated caves. On a busy day, all four trams and nine trailers are employed continuously, but come back from the caves empty as the passengers return by boat, underground, on the River Lesse which has just emerged into the open where the photograph is taken.

A steam tram in trouble with cows – who can't read plain French – on the metre-gauge Tramway Touristique de l'Aisne in the Ardennes. Belgium was once covered by a network of such lines (the SNCV or Vicinal) worked by steam trams, but most became electrified or dieselised and many have now closed altogether. Preserved examples of all three forms of traction are to be found on the line illustrated, which runs between Pont d'Erezée and Forge à la Plez.

Antwerp No.5348 gave 65 years of service before it was replaced by one of the modern bogie cars which now form the entire fleet. The tramway in one of Antwerp's central streets has recently been reconstructed in a subway.

**LUXEMBOURG** The Luxembourg city tram system was operated mainly by small, much-rebuilt four-wheelers like No.15, painted in a magnificent livery of dark blue and cream, with silver roof, gold lining and lettering, and dark green trucks. A narrow-gauge steam train once entered the city via the tram tracks and had to be preceded by a tram which actuated the points. Their last route was, alas, closed in 1964.

The old gave way to the new at Ghent in 1972 – elderly six-wheel tram No.331 is seen with one of the new Belgian-built 'PCC' type cars which now work the whole of the system.

**HOLLAND** An articulated interurban car towing an ex-steam trailer on the NZH company's system in The Hague. These 'Blue Trams' once ran on a succession of routes on differing gauges between The Hague, Amsterdam, and beyond, with town tramways at Leiden and Haarlem, but all have now succumbed to buses.

Heavy 'ironclad' interurban cars on three different routes at the Turfmarkt terminus in The Hague. The car in the centre once ran on the former Limburg tramways in the south-east corner of Holland, and returned there on display when no longer required in The Hague. It is now preserved in the Dutch railway museum at Utrecht. Modern trams now work two of the routes seen in the photograph, but the long route to Leiden has closed.

The Hague now has a
large fleet of these
'PCC' type cars, built in
Belgium to American
design but with body
modification to suit the
local operator.
Nos. 1173 and 1150 are
seen in 1959 when
quite new working in
multiple on a special
tour organised by the
Light Railway
Transport League.

One of the centre-entrance bogie cars that for many years were the backbone of the Rotterdam fleet. Apart from a few in reserve, they have now been replaced by articulated cars of the standard German Düwag design. The construction of a Metro line has resulted in a reshaping of the tramway system, and the routes south of the River Maas are now isolated. Car No.504 is seen at the former Lange Hilleweg terminus in 1959.

Amsterdam No.669 is one of a large number of modern three-section articulated cars which make up the tram fleet in the 'Venice of the North'. It is seen at Osdorp, on one of the several new routes that have been opened in Holland in the last few years.

**NORWAY** The once independent Ekebergbane operates into Oslo, starting off as a railway on private track and finally running through the city streets. It has now been absorbed into the city tram system, and the heavy bogie cars like No.1013 (appropriately painted battleship grey) have been put into reserve.

Although some of the Oslo trams have been replaced by suburban electric railways ('T-Banen'), several routes remain, operated by bogie cars such as Nos.226 and 228, seen here on the turning circle at Sinsen. The destination display is a model of clarity that could well be copied elsewhere.

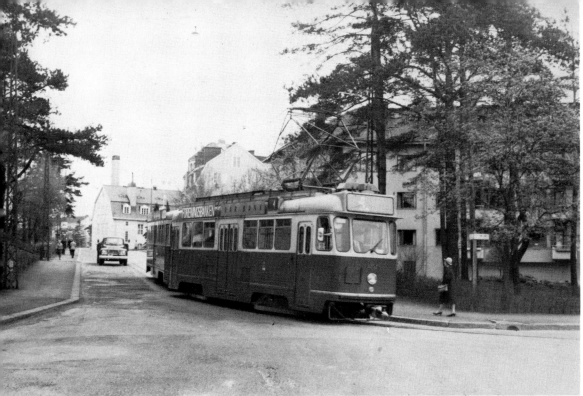

**FINLAND** The only trams remaining in this country are in Helsinki, but here we find a flourishing system worked mainly by modern bogie cars, recently supplemented by new articulateds which have displaced the last of the old four-wheelers. Bogie car 22 and trailer 512 are seen in the suburbs at Munkkiniemi.

One of Helsinki's old cars gained a new lease of life in the guise of an Advertising tram. Recent practice in some other countries has been to apply all-over adverts to a few cars in normal service.

**DENMARK** Copenhagen is wonderful no more for the tramway enthusiast, as its once-extensive system closed its last routes in 1972. These old cars had before then been replaced by modern German articulated cars, which in turn were sold to Egypt for further service in Alexandria. No tramways now remain in Denmark.

**SWEDEN** The tram system in the Swedish port of Malmo closed a few years ago, though one route survived the rule-of-the-road changeover in 1967. No.58 was a 'keep left' car which did not merit rebuilding.

Gothenburg has a large fleet of modern bogie cars, many built since 1967. Most of the tram routes in the city centre run through the streets, but in the suburbs are on reservations or private tracks, including sections in tunnel. Car No.760 is seen in the city centre, while No.582, working in multiple with two others, is seen at Hjallbo on one of the new extensions. 582 remains a left-handed car, and is coupled back-to-back with right-handed cars, to avoid running-round difficulties at temporary termini where there is no turning loop.

41

**WEST GERMANY**   The wartime standard car ('KSW' type), a four-wheeler with only twelve seats but large platforms and a high standing capacity, was supplied to many towns, but only a few of these cars now remain in service. No.61 is seen on a wintry day in Heidelberg, where a lot of them were built.

1926-vintage bogie car No.3 of the Esslingen-Nellingen-Denkendorf tramway, situated near Stuttgart, prepares to leave Esslingen for its run up the hill and into the country lanes. These cars still ran in 1975, but it is anticipated that they will soon be replaced – by what remains to be seen.

Ludwigshafen, an industrial centre on the Rhine opposite Mannheim, has only had its own tramway undertaking since 1965, the services previously being provided by Mannheim. Tram No.59 was built in the early 1950s when Germany was beginning to find her feet again after the war. The first post-war cars to be built incorporated parts from war losses ('Aufbau' type) but very similar cars ('Verbandstyp') were built new until outmoded by new designs in 1957.

Stuttgart is a very hilly city whose tramways are worked almost entirely by GT4 articulated cars. However, one oddity is route 30, which runs from Marienplatz to Degerloch up a steep rack section part of which is laid in the street. Six-wheeled, wide-bodied rack tram No. 105 dates only from 1950, but some of the trailers seen behind it at Degerloch were built in 1898.

The revolutionary Düwag 'Grossraumwagen' bogie cars supplied to many German systems in the 1950s replaced war losses and worn-out pre-war stock. Bremerhaven cars 79 and 215 were purchased from Offenbach when that town closed its tramway, and are seen at Parktor on Bremerhaven's only route.

The industrial town of Neunkirchen in the Saar is dominated by a steelworks in the town centre, and 'GT4' type articulated car No.5 is seen climbing the steep hill up to the suburbs. Although Neunkirchen only possesses seven trams, hundreds of this type of car operate in Stuttgart. They are products of the Esslingen factory, and are two-section cars on only two bogies.

A three-bogie, two-section articulated car with bogie trailer at Grünebergweg U-bahn station in Frankfurt. The Frankfurt subways were built for the 'Stadtbahn' (ie, city railway), but are served also by trams suitably modified for use at high platforms where necessary. The trams finish their journey on orthodox street or roadside track. Several German cities have realised the advantages of this type of operation, as well as others with purely tram subways, and purpose-built cars are now in production. The dividing line between railway and tramway becomes very hard to define in these conditions!

[J. F. Bromley]

Dortmund, justly famous for its breweries, has a large fleet of these three-section articulated cars on four bogies and driven from either end. Like No.34, they are painted in a distinctive livery of light brown, dark brown, and cream.

48

The ultimate in articulated cars is this five-section interurban car on six bogies, operated by the Rhein-Haardt Bahn which runs from Mannheim through Ludwigshafen and across country to the Spa town of Bad Dürkheim, whose main claim to fame appears to be its annual sausage festival.

A standard Bremen two-section, two-bogie articulated car built by Hansa in 1967. It is seen on a recent extension to a new housing development at Blockdiek and since the photograph was taken in 1968 further extensions have been opened.

**EAST GERMANY** Typical of the four-wheel trams and trailers operated by most German towns between the wars, these 1925-vintage cars in Karl Marx Stadt (previously known as Chemnitz) are however to the unusual gauge of 925mm, and are gradually being replaced by new Czech-built bogie cars on routes relaid to standard gauge. No.190 is seen at a newly-built tram station in the town centre, served by routes of both gauges.

Among the trams in this group at the Pillnitz terminus of the Dresden tramways is beautifully-restored 1902 car No.309 on a Light Railway Transport League special. The car on the left, No.1523, is one of the first post-war East German standard cars of which few now survive. Dresden have in recent years obtained Czech T4D bogie cars in large numbers to replace most older stock, and adopted the red and cream livery in which they are supplied as standard.

A three-car tram set in the modern surroundings of the rebuilt centre of East Berlin. The tram and its trailers are of the 'Reko' type, which utilised parts of older cars in their construction. They are to be found in large numbers in East Berlin, and in the last few years have also been built for provincial systems in East Germany. Note the computerised fleet numbers – a tram spotter's nightmare!

A works tram rebuilt from a passenger car heads a pair of modern bogie cars in the suburbs of East Berlin. The bogie cars bear a strong resemblance to those built in the 1950s in West Germany. Berlin of course became a divided city in 1945, and the tramways in the western sector have now all closed, being worked to the end by centre-entrance four-wheelers from the same series as the one seen here.

These four-wheel trams in Cottbus (not far from the Polish border) were built by the Czech Tatra factory to the designs of the Gotha works after it had ceased production. A large number of this type and its predecessors are to be found on almost every East German system, and a lot were also supplied to Russia. At the time CKD-Tatra took over production from Gotha, they had for several years already been producing technically far superior bogie cars, and as soon as existing orders were fulfilled, these cars began to appear in quantity in East Germany.

No.172 is one of the standard types built by the former Gotha factory in the early 1960s, and is an articulated car built on two rigid four-wheel trucks with a suspended centre-section. It is seen in the main square of Erfurt, a pleasant town in Thuringia, whose busy tram system is operated mainly by this type of car. The 'OS' in the first window indicates that the car is conductorless.

The Czech-built Tatra T4D-type bogie cars now form a large part of Magdeburg's fleet; they can work in multiple or with trailer. Due to sharp curves and tight clearances on some of the smaller East German systems, Tatra are producing a new design of articulated car to suit such conditions, and meantime the small towns soldier on with four-wheelers.

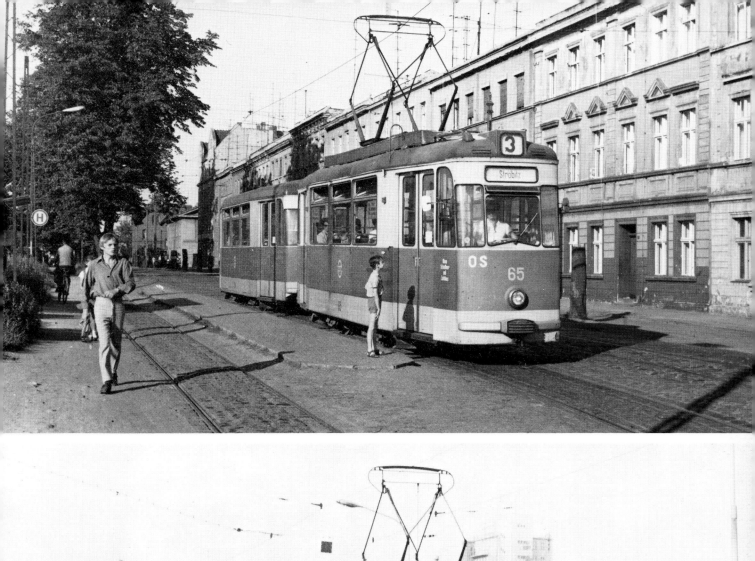

**AUSTRIA** A group of pre-war and post-war four-wheel cars on turning circles amid flower beds in front of the main station at Graz, a pleasantly-situated city in the south-east corner of the country. The preservation movement is very strong here, and examples of the principal types operated by the city have been restored both officially and privately.

The roads forming the Ring at Vienna are served by many tram routes which radiate thence to the suburbs. Vienna has a large fleet of modern trams in addition to the old cars of the type seen in the photograph, the newer cars being of virtually standard German Düwag design built in Austria under licence. Despite a number of route closures, Vienna remains one of Europe's largest tram systems, and now has some lengthy stretches of route in subways. [P. W. Gray]

Innsbruck, in the heart of the Tyrol, possesses two town routes worked by modern trams, and two country routes worked by very old stock. Car No.1 of the once-independent Stubaitalbahn (credited with being Europe's first A.C electric line) prepares to leave Innsbruck on its picturesque course up into the mountains to Fulpmes. Note the one-armed pantograph, incongruously fitted in the 1970s to the car which is otherwise virtually in 1904 condition.

The Postlingbergbahn is a metre-gauge line running up to the summit of the hill overlooking the city of Linz on the Danube. On warm days, old open-sided cars are brought into service, and car III (the fleet carries Roman numerals) is flying a white flag to denote that another car is following. The line is quite steep, and the cars are fitted with emergency brakes which grip the running rail. As a consequence, specially constructed points with no blades or frogs are used.

The short tramway connecting the town with the station at Gmunden is another part of the Stern & Hafferl empire, bogie tram No.8 being a solitary new car purchased in 1962. Although double-ended, it has doors on one side only.

The Stern & Hafferl company operate a number of light railways and tramways in the area west of Linz, and have an eye to secondhand bargains. Two ex-Dusseldorf metre-gauge bogie cars of 1935 vintage are seen at Vocklamarkt waiting to depart for Attersee.

**SWITZERLAND** Swiss standard bogie cars in Basle; these trams, some dating from the 1940s but others quite recently built, are to be found on the four principal Swiss tram systems – at Basle, Berne, Zurich and Geneva.

These four-wheel cars of 1910 vintage were still in peak hour service in Berne until as recently as 1972, and are typical of the stock which ran on most Swiss tramways until replaced by standard bogie cars.

Zurich No.1630 is one of 90 articulated cars obtained in 1966-8 together with a number of matching motorised trailers. They are rather unusual in being three-section cars with one bogie under each section. Livery is blue and white with silver roof, and like all Swiss trams, they are kept in immaculate condition.

Trams of two operators in Basle. No.301 of the city tramways together with No.13 of the Birseckbahn await departure on their interurban routes. This photograph was taken in 1967, and since then both operators have purchased new articulated cars, though bogie car No.13, a lively 60-year old, remains available for service.

Two trams in the Swiss mountains, on the Bex-Villars-Bretaye light railway. Through services on this line are worked by rack-fitted bogie railcars, but orthodox tramcars work local services through the streets on the adhesion sections of the line. Cars 9 (ex-Zurich) and 17 (ex-Lausanne) stand at Gryon, having worked along country roads from Villars. 17 is unusual in having a six-wheel truck.

**ITALY** Naples bogie car No.1005, dating from the 1930s and somewhat rebuilt, heads into the gloom of the Posillipo tunnel, one of two on the system which the trams share with other road users. This tram is in the dark and light green livery which was obligatory to Italian cities until a few years ago; most have now changed to a brighter and more visible livery, latest repaints in Naples being orange and grey.

Milan No.1881, one of 500 bogie cars ordered in 1928-30 based on an American design incorporating 'passenger-flow', with seated conductor. Milan has the largest tram system in Italy, and these cars still form the bulk of the fleet.

Turin rebuilt some bogie cars as articulateds in 1958-60, one such example being No.2812, seen passing through one of the arches in the picturesque city centre. Alone among the remaining Italian tram operators, Turin have so far retained the two-tone green livery.

One of a small number of articulated cars built new by the Breda factory for Milan in 1960, No.4733 is seen on the heavily-trafficked route 15. Three-section cars are currently being introduced in Milan, rebuilt from bogie cars, while new ones are on order.

The smallest Italian tram system is the Ferrovie del Renon, which runs high in the mountains above Bolzano in a part which once belonged to Austria. These trams formerly ran down a rack line into Bolzano piloted by an electric rack locomotive, but the rack line has now been replaced by an aerial cable railway, and two short tram routes run from the top of this to serve the mountain villages. Car No.12, seen here at Collalbo, and her sister No.11 are the last four-wheel trams in passenger service in Italy.

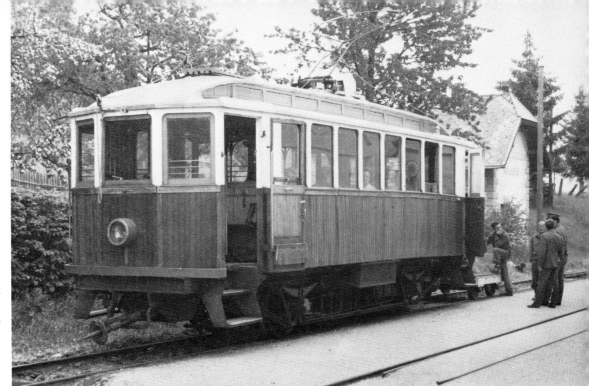

**GREECE** The only trams remaining in Greece are at the port of Piraeus, where a solitary route runs to Perama. This is possibly the least-visited tramway in Western Europe, one terminus being out of bounds to civilians! The service is worked by solid-looking bogie cars, but some older trams survive out of use, and are candidates for preservation. [A. Den Dulk]

**YUGOSLAVIA**   A powerful modern four-wheel car with two bogie trailers in the centre of Zagreb which, although Yugoslavia's second city, has its largest tramway system. Both cars and track are exceptionally well maintained, and the livery is a most attractive blue and cream. The cars in the photograph are among a large number built in the 1960s for Zagreb by Duro Dakovic of Slavonski Brod.

Sarajevo (where the assassination took place that sparked off the first world war) closed its 760mm gauge tram system in 1960, and replaced it with an extended standard gauge system, operated by 70 cars like No. 15, obtained secondhand from Washington, U.S.A! These cars are of the PCC type, an advanced design brought out in the 1930s following a conference of various American tramway company presidents, and built right up to 1952. Most of the surviving trams in the U.S.A. and Canada are of this type.

Osijek, in the north of Yugoslavia near the Hungarian border, is a small town which has only had an electric tramway since 1926 and these are two of the original trams. They have recently been replaced by Czech bogie cars.

**BULGARIA** The capital city of Sofia is the only tramway operator in the country, but has a large system to the unusual gauge of 1009mm which has been considerably extended in recent years and has received many new cars. The traditional three-car tramsets have been withdrawn since the photograph was taken, which shows car 122 at Parc Cristo Smiri in 1970.

**CZECHOSLOVAKIA** The city of Brno has a large tram system, and the older cars were very attractive, with varnished matchboarded sides, cream window surrounds, and large polished brass numerals. One such car was No.104, seen here at Obrany terminus on a miserable wet day in 1965. New bogie and articulated cars now provide the services in Brno, though a representative selection of old cars has been preserved, and a stretch of closed route retained *in situ* to run them on.

74

The Czech firm of CKD—Tatra built 771 trams of the T2 type in the late 1950s, about half going to Russia. Electrically and mechanically, they were very similar to the American 'PCC' type. In the photograph, No.222 is seen in Kosice, a city in eastern Slovakia with a tram system that has been much extended in the last decade due to industrial development.

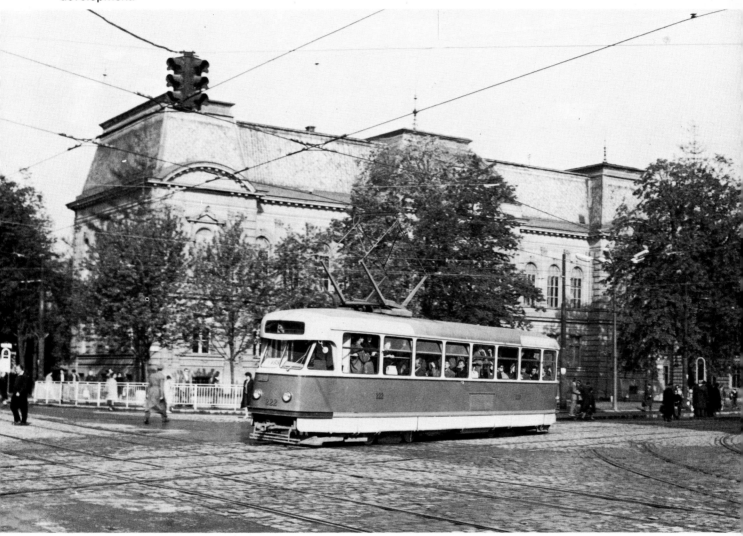

The tramways at Usti Nad Labem, on the River Elbe near the border with East Germany, closed in 1970. They were latterly worked mainly by 1948-built four-wheel cars of the Tatra 6MT type, such as No.107 in the photograph, together with an assortment of old and much rebuilt trailers. Their few modern cars have found new homes with other Czech tramways.

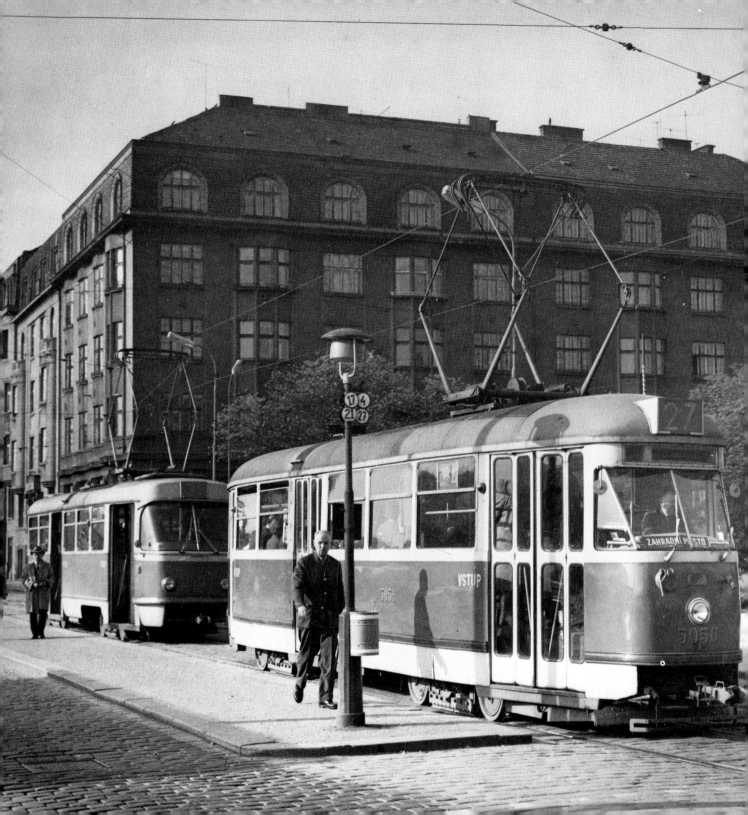

From 1960 to date, Tatra have produced the T3 type, a highly successful bogie car of which over 6000 have been built and are to be found all over eastern Europe. Prague No.6103, seen at Wenceslas Square in 1965, was one of the first production models. T3s often work in pairs and an articulated version, the K2, was produced only in comparatively small numbers, mainly for Russia.

The first CKD-Tatra production to incorporate the American 'PCC' features was the T1 type, of which less than 300 were built before being superseded by the T2. They were supplied to various Czech systems plus a few to Russia and Poland, who appear to have evolved their own variants. Although relatively new, several 'T1s' have already been scrapped or rebodied. No.5056 is seen in the suburbs of Prague, followed by a 'T3'.

77

**ROMANIA**   A large portion of what is now Romania formed part of Hungary prior to 1920. Sibiu, a small town near the foothills of the Transylvanian Alps, was in 1968 still operating trams which had once been Hungarian, such as Nos.6 and 12 and trailer No.14. This town must hold some sort of record, as for several years it had no less than four trams with the fleet number 14! However, most of their routes have now closed, and a few newer cars work the sole remaining route, which runs to the village of Rasinari.

Timisoara is another former Hungarian town now lying just inside Romania, and has a flourishing tram system with a good variety of cars. Old Ganz-built cars 112 and 111 are seen at Piata Libertatii, terminus of two single-track shuttle routes, but most of the system is double-tracked and worked by modern cars. Timisoara was a colourful place in 1968, as trams were then in three different liveries – red, yellow, or blue and cream.

Works trams are usually small four-wheelers, often converted from passenger cars, but at Bucharest in 1968 a number of these massive purpose-built bogie vehicles were running, carrying loads of hard core to tip on the site of a new depot.

A modern bogie car and four-wheel trailer at a suburban terminus in Bucharest which now possesses one of the largest tram systems in Europe. Note the unglazed second window – the glass is removed altogether from some windows in the hot Romanian summer, and it is not unusual to find a live pig as a travelling companion, or to be entertained *en route* by a blind musician with attendant urchin!

Bucharest has given many of its older cars a new lease of life by rebodying them. No.371 and trailers are seen here on one of the busy routes which pass close to, but do not penetrate, the main streets which form the city centre.

**POLAND**   When War broke out in 1939, a batch of trams for Warsaw was under construction at Chorzow in Silesia. The invading Germans seized these trams and ran them in Berlin, where many were destroyed. In 1945 the survivors finally reached their intended destination, and were known in Warsaw as the Pullman cars, being bigger and better than anything hitherto operated in that city. By 1974 the few survivors had been relegated to one route in the eastern suburbs, and renumbered with a '1' suffix to avoid a clash with new trams.                                                          [M. R. Taplin]

The old town in Warsaw, which was razed to the ground in 1945, has been completely and faithfully restored to its former glory, while modern motor and tram traffic has been diverted through a road tunnel under the area. Trams 776 and 95 are standard bogie cars of class 13N, part of a series of 843 almost identical trams delivered in 1959-70 which today make up the bulk of the Warsaw fleet. The design is very similar to the Czech Tatra T1.

[M. R. Taplin]

The German city of Breslau came under Polish administration from 1945 and has been renamed Wroclaw. The tramway system has been much modernised in recent years, and in 1974 the undertaking restored an old works car and trailer to turn-of-the-century condition for the operation of sightseeing tours. The cars are numbered 1 and 2 and given the names Jas and Malgosia (Hansel and Gretel). An understandable historical inaccuracy is the use of a Polish rather than a German company title.

[M. R. Taplin]

At the end of the war the new Polish administration adopted the German KSW (wartime utility) tram design as the basis for a standard car which could be built quickly and in large numbers for the ravaged tramway systems. Many thousands entered service, and Nos.301 and 592 seen here in the city centre of Poznan in 1974 represent the final version with automatic doors, that did not go out of production until 1959.    [M. R. Taplin]

Krakow, the ancient capital of Poland, has become an important industrial centre since 1945, and a complete new satellite town (Nowa Huta) has been built to house the expanding population. Tram route 4 linking the old and new cities is one of the most heavily used services in Poland, and requires three-bogie articulated trams running in multiple to handle the loads. Nos. 216 and 218 are of type 102Na built in 1970-2 while in the backgrounds are a pair of prototypes of type 102N. The scene is at Walcownia terminus in Nowa Huta in September 1974.
    [M. R. Taplin]

**HUNGARY** Debrecen, on the great Hungarian plain, has a number of these articulated cars built in 1961/2 in Budapest and supplied in small numbers to several provincial tram systems. The two end sections are carried on fixed four-wheel trucks, and the centre section is suspended. No.291 is on the trunk route which connects the station with the university via the city centre, and is seen in front of the Nagytemplom, a magnificent church which dominates the main square.

Hungarian cities make extensive use of the 'twin car', consisting of two old cars permanently coupled, each with controls removed from the inner ends. Thus there is no problem reversing cars at any required place on single-track routes. Budapest 2305 and 2304, dating from the early years of the century, are depicted at Rakosszentmihaly as recently as 1969.

A busy scene in
Budapest, at the
former Keleti terminus
of the interurban trams
which radiate out from
the city. Since the
photograph was taken
in 1968, this section
has been replaced by
an underground
railway, and the
terminus moved to a
point on the outskirts
of the city where
underground railway,
city trams, and
interurban trams all
interconnect. All these
three systems are now
under common
management.

Budapest lies on either side of the Danube; Buda, on the west bank is a hilly district, quite picturesque in parts, while Pest, on the east bank, is flat and largely industrialised. Many tram routes pass or terminate at Moscow Square in Buda, and in the foreground of the photograph are seen some of the fast and powerful bogie cars which operate in pairs with an intermediate trailer on the busiest routes.

Modern articulated cars such as No.1310 have been produced for Budapest in some quantity from 1967 onwards, and have replaced many of the old four-wheelers which used to abound in the city.

These distinctive Budapest centre-entrance cars with their deep domed roofs date from 1928-30, and when this picture was taken in 1964 were still to be found on busy routes in the city centre. Their days are now practically finished, and the last survivors are confined to a short route in the suburbs.

**RUSSIA** There are over 110 tramway operators in the Soviet Union, many of them rarely if ever visited by enthusiasts. Our selection of views are all taken in Leningrad, which boasts the world's largest tramway system, and where every year sees the opening of new extensions to keep pace with the expansion of the suburbs. Trackwork borders on the extravagant and every terminus has separate tracks for each service. This scene at Svetlanovski in the far north shows the immediate pre-war and post-war tramcar designs.                                [M. R. Taplin]

As befits the world's largest tramway, Leningrad also has the greatest number of trams of any one type on any one system, the LM57 class, of which 1000 were built in 1957-66. This wintry scene in February 1974 shows 5747 running through the woods on the main road south from the city.   [M. R. Taplin]

In 1967, car 5210 was rebuilt as a prototype for a new class of tramcar which eventually materialised as the LM68 type. Finding the odd car out on a system with about 2300 trams is quite a task, but in February 1974 our intrepid photographer ran 5210 to ground on route 43 working from Varshavski Voksal.

[M. R. Taplin]

The Leningrad winters are severe and snowstorms are frequent, but the citizens are masters at the art of wrapping up well, and can even be seen enjoying ice creams at times like this. The scene is Ploshad Stachek terminus in the southern suburbs, and No.3539 with its matching trailer are of type LM47 which came from the Riga carriage works in 1948.

[M. R. Taplin]

In 1966-7 Leningrad conducted a brief experiment with articulated trams, but only four of these three-bogie cars of class LVS66 emerged from the Yegorov factory. All four can be seen on route 19, and each carries a different livery. No.1002 looks very smart in cream with blue trim as it rolls along Obvodny Street.

[M. R. Taplin]

The longest route in Leningrad is the interurban line to Strelna, about 25km from the city centre to the south-west. Even this service rates a car every ten minutes, and there are several short workings to intermediate termini such as Bulvarnoya. Cars 6018 and 6019 are of the modern LM68 type which generally operate in multiple units of two.

[M. R. Taplin]

There are still about 200 pre-war trams in Leningrad large bogie cars dating from 1933-6 which are noticeably noisier than their modern counterparts. Motor cars carry odd numbers, trailers even numbers, Nos.4393 and 4326 being photographed in February 1974 on a new extension to Sosnovaya Polyana where the terminus is a large single-track loop around modern flats built in a clearing in the forest.                                                                                                [M. R. Taplin]